Presented To:

_____

From:

_____

Date:

_____

Message:

_____

_____

_____

_____

_____

_____

10,000

STEPS
TOWARDS
ME

A guide to your personal development journey

Anna Ngarachu

Copyright and Credits © 2021 Anna Ngarachu

ISBN: 978-0-620-91995-1 (print)

Cover Designer: Motsanaphe Morare

Editor and Proof-reader: Sonia Soneni Dube

This book was published by
the Golden Goose Institute (Pty) Ltd

For further information
email: info@thegoldengooseinstitute.com

DEDICATION

To all the big dreamers searching and moving
towards their true north and who want to live
an authentic life, not only for themselves but for
the benefit of those around them.

ACKNOWLEDGMENTS

To my family, whom these stories would not have panned out without. To the eight 'musketeers' who keep bringing more memories I can work with. We have a great journey ahead of us, together.

To Grant, thank you for paving the way for my author journey and for your endless guidance. Your belief is unbounded.

To my English teachers for teaching me to "engage with the text". It has sparked my love for writing.

To my business coaches, mentors, and the books and audios in the self-development space: without this community, I would have never developed my mindset and grown to lead and teach others through my writing.

To all those who moved me closer to who I am today, and healed me along the process, you are special.

To my reviewers and editors thank you for engaging and adding your colour to my work.

FOREWORD

The year is 2004 and I have just completed my O-Level exams. I am 16 at the time and my plan is to become a medical doctor by the time I am 25. I will also be married by then and be considered to fall in the same tax bracket as Richie Rich.

It is 2021 as I write this. I am not a doctor. I own a publishing and self-development company; I am a qualified life and body coach; a professional speaker, and; an author of three books. I am also madly in love with the woman of my dreams, and I am eating healthy and exercising regularly. I am just not in Richie Rich's tax bracket yet, but I am in full confidence that I am on the right path.

You may ask, "What happened between 2005 to 2021?"

Let me tell you.

By 2013, I had been to two universities: The University of Namibia, where I started studying a BSc in Computer Engineering, which morphed into a BSc in Computer Science because I had failed my engineering modules in my first year. Computer Science was no different. I met a stumbling block called calculus which let me know abstract numbers and I were not the best of friends.

Eventually, I leave Namibia and go to South Africa and begin my journey again at the University of South Africa. I remember registering for Accounting Science with the dream of becoming a Chartered Accountant but by the time I am done with my first year, I have a stark realisation; Economics is more my forte. So, by 2013 I graduate with my Economics degree and in 2020, I finally complete my Postgraduate Diploma in Investment Planning with the University of Free State.

When I used to reflect on the years between 2004 to 2021, I would look at them as years of failure. I had a disdain for myself and my lack of discipline to decide and execute accordingly. I know what you are thinking, "But Grant, you met the love of your life, you are working towards financial freedom, you have written three books, and you are working on your fourth. Oh, and you are healthy too! Lack of discipline? I don't know about that." You have chosen to see the glass half full; I however am questioning why the glass was never full, to begin with.

After 17 years I now have an answer. This answer was birthed from intentional daily reflection and articulated brilliantly by reading the book you are now holding. I was taking 10,000 steps towards myself. I was getting to know who Grant Senzani truly was and began building towards who Grant Senzani is and who he will become. Not the Grant Senzani he would like people to fall in love with, be in awe of or give respect to but rather, the Grant Senzani he gets to look at in the mirror and love for simply being himself.

It has not been the easiest of journeys, but it certainly has been the most fruitful.

The book you are now holding in your hand, I can vouch will guide you to your authentic self. What took me 17 years to learn, will take you less than 30,000 words to obtain by simply reading and going through the exercises.

This book will begin to shed light on who you truly are and ensure you take active steps in choosing your next steps from the foundations of self-awareness and authenticity. The author, Anna Ngarachu, takes you on this journey by holding your hand and sharing the experiences that have led her to where she is now. Her perspective is birthed from her experiences, how she took her path to find herself, what prompted it, and how you may now do the same if you choose to.

I have published tons of books and I have read kilotons of books. This one is different because this one is about you and becoming more of you.

Enjoy the journey and all the growth it will come with.

Grant Senzani
Entrepreneur, Author, and Speaker.

REVIEWS

"Aptly as the book begins, *10,000 Steps Towards Me* is like settling in for a much-needed catch up with an old friend. It is filled with pearls of wisdom and charming anecdotes that are so… Authentically Anna! I would surely pick this one off the shelf to read on a self-care day! The stories are relatable and uplifting, like a soul-soothing balm of self-love. A real gem from a charismatic and powerful woman."

—Mohini Pillay
Artist & Entrepreneur.

"So often, within the chaos of life, we lose touch of personally growing and defining our lives. The tragedy is a busy life instead of a purposeful life. This book is full of wisdom and practical application on getting back to building the right foundation for a purposeful life. I've had the privilege of walking a few of the 10,000 steps of Anna's journey - she writes with the same transparency and wisdom that she lives by. It has equipped me and will continue to be a reference as I face the journey ahead."

—**Carly-Marie van Niekerk.**

"Anna allows us to understand and unpack the things that disconnect us from our true selves. She asks incisive questions that urge you to reflect before moving on to the next chapter. This book gets you to take the steps necessary to prepare for the life you want, the work environment/ business venture you want, and even the life partner you desire. Her storytelling is engaging which allows you to be drawn towards the experiences shared. We get to create our stories and own every facet of them. This book would be a great 'intended gift' for anyone who dares to change."

—**Luyanda Dlamini**
DTM, Entrepreneur, Author of What Had Happened Was… How to Build Inner Strength When Your World Crumbles.

"A truly remarkable book, overflowing with stories that are relatable and which holds a beautiful mixture of humour and optimism that immediately stretches you and inspires you to do more. Unlike most self-improvement books, this one targets an infinite array of areas in which you can, and ultimately must improve, presented through the unique random flow of the writing."

—Maraliza C Leyds
Friend, Facilitator, Attorney.

"The book *10,000 Steps Towards Me* by Anna Ngarachu is a must-read for anyone on the journey to self-discovery, whether young or old. The author has obviously done extensive research on the topics covered in this book and provides very personal accounts from her own life which allows the reader an opportunity to be vulnerable, honest, and reflective about his/her own life-changing events. The book is easy to read and is warm and comfortable."

—Sindzisa Mbhalati
Engineer, Entrepreneur, Career Coach.

"Why live a haphazard life when you can take 10,000 steps to become all that you were born to be? Life, however, is not perfect and bad things do happen to good people too. We may not be able to control everything that happens to us, but we can certainly control how we react to them. Becoming You is the best gift you could ever give this world."

—Mandy Petrus
Co-Author of 'Believe Again: A Journey of Hope'.

"This book is for anyone on the path to self-discovery. An approachable read with practical questions for self-evaluation, helping you move towards who you want to be and what you want to achieve."

—Chandre Combrinck
Connector, Coffee Lover, Business Enthusiast.

"A beautiful collection of nostalgic stories, coupled with practical tools to reflect and direct you towards your own journey of self-discovery and self-awareness. An authentic recollection and masterpiece."

—Michael Ngarachu
Personal and Executive Coach, Performance Coach.

"The real beauty of this book is its authenticity. If you want to walk 'the road less travelled' towards your unique future these twelve lessons will impact you. If you long to develop your authentic self, Anna's *10,000 Steps Towards Me* will provide liberating insights to assist you."

—Dr. Ruth M Greeff – *MBH Ph.D.*

CONTENTS

PROLOGUE

So it's that time of the year again where everyone is looking to set you up with this friend, or that cousin, and at this point, you're certainly over it. All your previous blind dates didn't go anywhere, including that proposal to your ex – we will not get into those details. Not to mention the job interview that you completely botched. It's been a rough year, enough said. However, you keep going back and forth trying to pinpoint what the issue has been – why didn't you connect with anyone at all? How come it seems that you cannot figure out the job thing? This was not like you; you were a magnet back in high school. Has life suddenly eroded all your charm?

So you set up a call with your old college buddy, Sophia, to run through your difficulty with connecting with people lately. She knew you when you guys were kids and you believe she is the person who is the most likely to be completely honest with you. So, you book a table at Olives and Plates, like in the old days, and confirm via WhatsApp. Tomorrow is the day for answers.

It's been such a long time since you've caught up with Sophia. The smell of the roasted coffee and omelettes are pungent this morning and from the view above the Hyde Park skyline, it looks like it will be a warm summer. You sip your chai latte slowly, savouring the delicate hazelnut flavour that you asked the waitress to add. They are not used to such a particular customer like you. The waiter asks you for your breakfast order and the croissants arrive warm and melted with chocolate; just the way you like them.

As you dig into your food, you recall when you and Sophia used to come up with all sorts of stories and theories about things; most of them deep thoughts, while others were very fleeting. You can't wait to reconnect with her. In the corner of your eye, you see her approaching. She still walks at her upbeat jovial pace and makes eye contact with everyone, making one feel like they are the most important person around.

So midway through the chocolate-filled croissant, after an hour of catching up, you make that pensive face you always do and say to Sophia, "Soph, you've known me a long time, and I want your honest take on this." She places her cappuccino down, unfazed, and intertwines her fingers, leaning her chin against them ready for another one of your deep conversations.

"Yes friend, what seems to be the problem?" Sophia asks.

"Well, I've been having trouble connecting with people lately or even pursuing the ideas that I wanted to." You relay your countless bad date encounters; inability to choose your new career path, and; the constant feeling of indecision.

Sophia, privileged to be the one you're being vulnerable to, stops and asks you, "I hear what you're saying, but what is it that you want? What is it that you want in a partner? What do you want to do when you wake up each day?"

Swallowing your sparkling water rather uncomfortably, you utter, "I really don't know".

"Then if you don't know what you want, how can you know what to ask for?" she responds.

"Then I guess I better figure that out," you attest.

"Yes, you need to, dear."

"How come you look like you have it all put together though Soph?" you ask honestly.

"Well, I don't have it all figured out. I'm working on that everyday... For me figuring out what I wanted, in different aspects of my life didn't come easily actually. You remember what a mess I was back in college. But what I did is to take time to reflect on WHO I really was, and then after that, I could chart the path of figuring out WHAT I wanted. Obviously what we want can change, but knowing you and connecting with yourself is a good starting point to building an authentic life... I know that's a mouthful."

"No, no... that's very interesting and insightful, please go on. I need to do that too. Where do I start though?" you ask curiously.

"Well, there are many ways to do many things... I just got some help along the way by reading books and getting out of my head and opening up to new ideas. Mind you, there is an excellent book that helped me. So much so that I made a point to attend the author's book launch and meet her. I got like three copies! It's called umm… how can I forget - *'10,000 Steps Towards Me'*. I'll drop you a copy and we can chat more?"

"You have no idea how much that would help!" you attest, glad that you took the first step to get some answers.

Excitedly Sophia begins to unravel aspects of this book, her eyes lighting up and her heart full of wisdom. "The author starts with this whole idea of self-discovery being a puzzle… She touches on family – you know how our families can either make or break us? Ooh! There's even a section on finding one's life partner that may save you from more bad dates."

You both laugh out loud.

And so here we are…

INTRODUCTION

*"[Our] main task in life is to give birth to
[ourselves] to become what [we] potentially [are]."*
—Erich Fromm

Have you ever looked in the mirror and thought, "Yes, this is me." I mean truly knowing who you are; and even though you may not know what your purpose in life is, you have a starting point which is that you know yourself well. I argue that even if we know ourselves well, there is always a lot more to learn.

If you're a lot like most people, then finding out who the real you is may have been a process of discovery, and it may still be a journey right now. Well welcome, you have come to the right place! You have found another person (me!) just like you who's been on a similar journey and is still journeying on the path of self-discovery... finding my authentic self. It feels like a never-ending process and a bit like a puzzle but slowly, we figure out the pieces.

I'm going to tell you a story about my journey. It is about me getting to know who I am over a period of time and through a variety of occasions and circumstances. I know the concept of finding our true selves may sound a little contorted, but I assure you, it's definitely not as mind-bending as a Christopher Nolan film. I'm going to share my story and the lessons I learnt along the way that built me up into the person I am today. The focus here is on the lessons learnt which I hope will help you in your personal development journey. I don't have it all figured out, maybe some of you have, but I hope it will challenge some of your thinking, inspire you to take the time to develop yourself, and move you to do the same in someone else's life. So come, take a walk with me... let's get to 10,000 steps together.

Where Does Our Journey Start?

Our process of self-discovery is shaped by certain life events, the things we come across, and the people who influence our lives. It can often be a puzzle. Life and people along the way have an influential impact on our lives. Why is self-discovery so important? It's because we want to ensure we are living a life that is true to who we are and fulfils us in that regard. All too often we hit stumbling blocks that lead us to question ourselves, our value systems, and where we are headed in life. I call these stumbling blocks 'disconnects' because they either disconnect us from our true selves or create doubt about the path we're meant to take. We often find that these disconnects can be monsters in our hearts and ones that we are constantly trying to battle.

My journey is framed through some of these disconnects that caused me to waiver in my self-discovery process, and the lessons I learnt that would help me overcome them and steer me back towards my true self. Some of these disconnects I believe you can most certainly relate to, and I urge you to focus on the lessons learnt as there are some gems that have guided me and may just work for you too. These disconnects are the subtitles of each chapter, and the titles have a creative spin encompassing the general theme of the chapter.

I pick a few disconnects that stuck out to me through my journey from childhood into adulthood. Obviously, there are several other stumbling blocks out there but I chose to pick these as they were pertinent for me. There is no particular order to these disconnects, and so the chapters are not in any chronological order, as these causes can occur at various stages of one's life and differ for each person.

If you picked up a book like this, then finishing a book of this nature will come easily. So read it throughout. You can start with whichever chapter you like, although I did write the book from early memories to latter ones; either way, each chapter will come together to a powerful conclusion with some takeaway ideas to navigate these stumbling blocks in our lives. I believe this book needed to be written. You and I have been waiting to read something like this all along.

For those who would like to skip right ahead and work on the reflective exercises that will help you uncover who and what has been influencing your ability to live authentically, jump into my framework tool: *A dozen reflective doses - Take the quiz!*

I would like to hear some of the reasons that caused you to question who you are. Feel free to write to me at anna@impactstoryteller.co.za. I am always keen to indulge in your story.

As you navigate the book you will also understand why I had to write it. In summary, there were too many wise ways I had discovered to see the world and navigate it, through reading personal development material growing up - not just any material, but from the 'Greats' (Napoleon Hill and the likes). I had to share it. I thought that if this stays in my head, it will only be accessible to a few select people. How do I simplify what I've experienced in my life but discuss it in a way that anyone can understand and relate with, without discounting the depth of the concepts? That was the challenge I set for myself with this book. I then decided to dedicate my lockdown year (2020) to write this book.

This is my first published book – but believe me, there will be more as I pivot to my niche area of creative writing.

My hope for you is to use these stories and points as a guide for your personal discovery and personal development journey. I hope that the steps I have taken and lessons I have learnt can help you reflect on your life and come to the realisations that you seek. I hope some of the humorous stories (and some of the deep ones) move you enough to act. To act positively towards finding who you truly are and take the leap to live an authentic life; one that is unique to you, as it will be the most original story out there! I can't wait to hear about your journey of discovery.

HOMES VERSUS HOUSES

*"In every conceivable manner, the family is a link to
our past, bridge to our future."*
—Alex Haley

Point of departure

There is a funny thing about houses. They can
bring back all sorts of memories, good, bad and
ugly but at the end of the day, they remain
somewhat of a haunting presence in our minds.
I remember the second home we lived in; it was
in a beautiful estate in Runda, Nairobi. That's
me in the picture below as a little girl among the
roses. It was home for a long time but now it's a
house with lots of partial hazy memories. The
house was surrounded by all sorts of flowers

and lawns that encircled it like a moat. It was the most beautiful place I can remember as a child, given I had not seen too many things before the age of ten. It always brought me peace and serenity.

Anna in her home garden in Nairobi

As my memory evades me, what stood out for me in that house were the interactions among me and my siblings which made it home for me. I can recall us coming from school and having a snack. Food was either lavish or simple; sometimes it was rice and milk (yeah, when you have six kids simple is king), and when it was lavish, it was when the chef cooked dinners for us. Yes, you heard right - chef. I can't remember how long Paulo stayed with us or what he used to cook but it was a three-course feast and being under 10, that was a sumptuous meal fit for a queen. I really think that was the point when I developed my love for food - not just any food, Paulo-standard food. So, one can only imagine the growth of my stubbornness around food. I could quickly discern well-made versus average food. So when I had to eat ugali and sukumawiki (pap and kale) I sneered, only internally so that I didn't get into trouble. I have carried that sneering with me and boy do I not cook pap and kale anymore! Looking back, I believe I made the right choice as I soon realised how refined pap was not the best choice for one's diet. So maybe I had a nose not only for quality as a kid but the healthy stuff too. That's my excuse anyway…

As kids, we also came up with all sorts of games, from hopscotch to hide and seek… and then we adopted rabbits too as our fellow playmates. Unfortunately, the rabbits did not last long enough for our games; there is still some mystery as to how they perished - not sure if it was the cat or one of my brother's tactics that led to their premature demise. Naturally, we built standards in our childhood, where spending time with each other was how we entertained ourselves. That has carried on into adulthood and my siblings and I are still the best of friends and we choose to hang out with each other as often as possible. The three musketeers, my three younger brothers, and the last two youngest additions who learnt to send emojis way too soon - remain completely inseparable. This, therefore, made me very family-oriented.

A leaf from my life

Family upbringing can be a significant determinant of our habits, values, and mindsets. To illustrate a habit from childhood and my strong value system for non-conformity is a funny story I recall between me and my mother… episodes of the early morning rush to school.

I have never been one to wake up super early. I'm not sure why because this was the case even when I was probably five or so. I remember how my mother would dutifully wake us up to go to nursery school, and on one particular day I was being especially stubborn; going in and out of my bed so that my brain could eventually wake up. I also remember pots and pans being bashed; there may have been splashes of water on my face but my body was not having it. All I kept wondering was why I was being tortured. I complied by crawling out of bed and getting dressed in my pink kindergarten uniform. Once breakfast was done, it was time to head to school. My mother mentioned something about a sweater, and because I felt that I had given in to a lot that day, I said, "No, I don't need one." Then a war started.

I've still never understood why mothers feel colder or warmer than us (and hungrier now that we're at it). Why did I need to go to school with a sweater when I wasn't feeling cold? Why couldn't I be the one to decide? All of a sudden, I remember someone saying, "The police are here!" The horror! Why would anyone call the cops on a little angel? Have they not seen what kind of girl I am? (See my picture in the flowers above). I cannot remember if this was accurate, but I definitely saw some blue and red lights by the gate when I stepped out of the house briefly. I was being threatened to go to school wearing a sweater…

I tell this story as a humorous one because I cannot confirm nor deny whether it actually took place. However, I recall many times being made to do this and that ahead of going to school which didn't end well for me. I ended up disliking being told what to do and the whole idea of conformity. Don't get me wrong, I love education and I was the curious creative kid; I just didn't like going to a place with my pink uniform, where someone would also tell me what to do and subsequently, what and how to learn.

This perspective has been cemented in me, which explains why I didn't like going to primary school either, nor university, or even why I didn't enjoy getting up in the morning to go to work. High school was a bit better as I enjoyed certain aspects of it because it allowed me to discover my creative talents. I believe I have realised the reason behind this. It's because I believe I can live an unconventional life; work for myself, from where it best suits me; learn my interests; and finally live a life that fulfils me, and even pursue my passions! This is something that I have strongly realised about myself which was not particularly stressed by those around me whilst I was growing up.

This mindset is a gift in that I can see beyond the average everyday monotony, strongly holding on to the belief that I can create a life I envision and do the activity to someday create it. However, it has also caused a lot of tension wherever I go, because what I've realised is because I know how I want to live my life and I'm willing to fight for it, I see things very differently and also do things differently to others. This is the case as far as the people I choose to hang with and the person I've chosen as my life partner are concerned. I have had to leave a couple of people in my life behind and take a different path, which as a young person has not been easy because I felt I would miss out on all the fun! Bless those people, I still love them and have no bitterness towards them. It is just that my road was taking me elsewhere and I had to get onto that path.

So even though I have had to get a job and learn in a career, whilst pursuing my business interests and finding my creative path in life, I know that I will have to leave behind certain aspects once my path is clear to take me to where my true passions lie.

Point to ponder

Have you ever felt that there is more to your life and are you wondering whether you are ready to start creating it? Have you felt that the mindset you were brought up with may not align with you – could there be more?

Write out your reflections:

....

....

....

....

....

....

....

....

....

....

....

Homes Versus Houses

....

....

....

....

....

....

....

....

....

....

....

....

....

....

....

....

....

....

....

....

....

Driving the point home

How you were brought up, or your childhood years, will either align with your true sense of identity or it may cause some sort of disconnect because it may lead you to question who you are. This may be because you don't align with some of the value systems that were around you.

For me, my childhood years revealed to me why family is such an integral part of my life and that's been a value system going into adulthood because it aligns with my true self.

However, my upbringing, from the schools I attended to the people that were meant to be example characters, also led me to think in a particular way. For example, I grew up with the narrative of 'be a good girl, be a good student, study hard (all the time), get a good job, and you should be okay'. These are all good traits of course but over time, I realised that I did not align with this linear thought process of just studying and getting a job because I knew there was more to life than that.

At that time, there were not many advocates for entrepreneurship or people telling me that I could live out my passions. This was years ago and that mental process has changed, but the past is ingrained until we overcome it. I felt that there were many more options in life and that I could follow my passions and be my own boss someday, somehow, and that conforming to the predominant thinking of those around me was not the be-all-and-end-all. I knew that I wanted something different in life and so I had to change some of those thinking habits. Does anyone relate?

Key takeaways

Firstly, I have learnt that family will always be there for you, in their own way, even if they have different viewpoints. The point is that your dream and how you want to live your life is YOURS. It doesn't belong to anyone else; not your parents, not your siblings, and not your in-laws either. You were put on this earth to fulfil your purpose. There is a brilliant poem, *"On Children"* by Kahlil Gibran, that depicts how unique each of us and our dreams are, and the fact that we, as individuals, do not belong to anyone, and neither do our dreams.

And a woman who held a babe against her bosom said, Speak to us of Children.

And he said:

Your children are not your children.

They are the sons and daughters of Life's longing for itself.

They come through you but not from you,

And though they are with you yet they belong not to you.

You may give them your love but not your thoughts,

For they have their own thoughts.

You may house their bodies but not their souls,

For their souls dwell in the house of tomorrow, which you cannot visit, not even in your dreams.

You may strive to be like them, but seek not to make them like you.

For life goes not backward nor tarries with yesterday.

You are the bows from which your children as living arrows are sent forth.

The archer sees the mark upon the path of the infinite, and He bends you with His might that His arrows may go swift and far.

Let your bending in the archer's hand be for gladness;

For even as He loves the arrow that flies, so He loves also the bow that is stable.

Yes, we may grow up in homes that we want to break out of because they are toxic, or want to remain there forever because they are our safe havens. Regardless, there comes a point when you need to take your own path that is true to you. It is always gracious and sensible to communicate what you are about to do (if it is safe to do so) to your family because you care about them, not because they need to approve it. Remember, advice from people is often an expensive thing; easily handed out but you and I are the ones that have to carry the consequences of that advice.

I have also learnt that sometimes in our life journeys we may learn some new values that we would need to teach our families. Remember, they are probably operating from the conditionalities of their parents too, which may be outdated and off-centred at times. So it is okay to teach new values to those around us. As an example, I wanted to share the concepts of dream building and understanding personalities with my family, that I had learnt and were useful, and I did this by sharing books and material with them. This was because I wanted to understand everyone around me better because growing up, communication did not come by easily especially between myself, as a child, and my parents.

To be able to communicate with my family better, I set out on a path to learn about personalities. Yes, families can be difficult to get through to but eventually, over time they come around. Books and media were an instrument I could use, instead of it sounding as if I was the one telling people what to do. I first had to understand myself and then the uniqueness of each member of my family. Now, I can relate to them much better, but first I had to understand myself.

Why this was important to me was because as a child growing up, I felt like I was a tyrant at times. I had a very detailed personality and could be quite commanding sometimes, but I had no idea why. I then realised it was my personality trait, among other suppressed anger issues inside, that I eventually had to deal with.

I was then able to better understand my strengths and weaknesses and tune them appropriately so I could be the best version of myself, towards those I cared for the most. And naturally, I wanted to bless my family with this gift.

I have also learnt to meet people where they are at, and accept who they are. For example, years later, my dad shared personality tests with us, for us to test ourselves too. Inside, I was nodding and acknowledging that we were now on the same page.

So choose love at the end of the day as a way to relate with family and find your alignment from a loving point of view. Our families teach us values that will be imprinted on us throughout our lives. It is important to keep the good ones and build on those, and change those value systems that may have not been so gracious, so we can propel ourselves forward wisely and authentically. To be able to operate from a viewpoint of love, we must heal inside as well, as we cannot give what we don't have either.

THE GOOD, THE BAD, AND THE UGLY[1]

EXTRANEOUS CIRCUMSTANCES AND THEIR INFLUENCE ON YOU - WHEN 'LIFE HAPPENS'

"I never lost faith in the end of the story."
—Admiral Jim Stockdale

Point of departure

If you're like me, you're probably not a fan of the phrase 'life happened' because it just highlights a time you had to accept things as they were and you couldn't change the situation; you were not in control.

I came across a spiritual understanding of this phrase in early 2020 that I have to include here. You see, a lot of us grew up with the belief that good and bad things taking place were transactional: if you were good to the best of your ability then good things would flow to you, while if you lived unfavourably then bad things would happen to you. The reality we come to terms with eventually, is that bad things happen to good people too. Both bad and good things are all part of nature, the circle of life.

For many, this reality has caused them to lose faith in their worldview and spirituality. Internally, growing up, I had accepted this harsh truth. However, it didn't quite make sense to me logically and so I continued to battle with this concept for years until I recently listened to a sermon by Andy Stanley[2] on the matter. As I am no pastor, nor can I articulate myself as well as Andy on the matter, I challenge you to listen to it, whether you are spiritual or not. For we don't know what we don't know. I learnt the concept of the global consequence of sin which meant that despite the good in this world, when sin entered the world, with it came a myriad of larger consequences like death. With this global consequence, even you and I are not immune to its effects. This doesn't mean we live a life of fear; it just means that we cannot lose our faith or beliefs because of these consequences. We cannot lose our faith in the end of the story. This is how Andy frames his sermon, around Admiral Jim Stockdale's saying, who was the highest-ranking US military officer to be imprisoned in the "Hanoi Hilton" war camp during the Vietnam War.

I mention the above to frame this next chapter. It's not an easy one to talk about, neither is it easy to relive as I write it. I know burying the past may be a useful strategy but it is only temporary. I trust this brings hope for you who've had to undergo similar circumstances; to confront and deal with your own story and move forward having learnt something from it. And for my family, it is important to own our truth, regardless of how bitter it may have been. Then only can we move on after beating the dust that layered on us.

A leaf from my life

I think I was about nine years old when I began to notice a fundamental rift between my parents. I was too young to read any red flags but I knew that reduced conversations and increased confrontations over some time were not normal for a couple. Perhaps I was too observant, however, I was not able to express what I noticed to anyone because I felt I had no voice. As a little girl, what clout did I have to voice my opinion or to suggest that a sit-down intervention was necessary?

The episodes that took place eventually led to what is known as a temporary separation between my parents – these events were not clear to me and remain unclear today. Again, I didn't know exactly what was going on. In those days, it also seemed taboo to mention what was going on to others, so as to gather some explanation. I didn't understand the term taboo then, but that was the aura around the subject. Yes, so my parents got divorced; and between the time I was 9 and 15 years old, it would be a rocky part of our lives.

Throughout that whole ordeal, I found that I had to grow up quickly and become what I term a 'second mum' for my brothers. This created a large burden in the sense that I felt that I had to take care of everyone. As a result, I have always wanted to beat back into the past and be 15 again. Why 15? Well, that was the point when I felt the least burden on my shoulders and started to emerge as an individual; not as a sister who had to protect and care for her siblings or a good student, but just me. I carried this sense of wanting to take care of everyone into my adult years, and had to deal with and let go of it eventually.

When I was 15 years old, we were also living in Uganda, which took some time to get accustomed to but when I did, it was the utter semblance of blissful living. Those three years in Uganda provided an opportunity for healing and normality. As soon as I had started understanding myself, and finding my voice, no sooner did it feel like it was being taken away when we had to move to South Africa. That took a lot of getting used to as well, as things had to change. Leaving my friends in Uganda was not easy. Leaving a school that understood and appreciated my creativity was not great, and moving into a blended family out of the blue required great tolerance and eventually, acceptance. However, South Africa became the place I would become an adult and learn about the world. So, yes there is a special place South Africa still holds in my heart. It is still home even today.

Point to ponder

What event has dramatically shaped your life, and thrown you off course a little or in a major way? Has this event caused you to question who you are, what you want to do, and your value system?

Write out your reflections:

....

....

....

....

....

....

....

....

....

....

....

....

....

....

....

....

....

....

....

....

....

....

....

....

....

....

....

....

....

....

....

....

....

....

....

....

....

....

....

Driving the point home

We can all talk about one or a couple of events that have influenced us. Reflecting on these situations and how they impacted how we think and who we have become is important. Is a certain event continuing to impact you negatively? What type of change would you like to see in yourself going forward? What positive thing can you do to help you move forward?

Well, obviously for me, my parents' divorce had a major impact on my life. How I would come to view relationships and marriage, and whether I could trust people, for example, were tested and I have had to attain my definition of these elements. Trusting people easily was definitely impacted but I have made amends and attempts to work on myself despite all that happened.

Good things and bad things happen to everyone; it's not transactional, it's just part of life. Certain events in our lives will shape our perspective on how we see people, and whether we trust them and their actions. This event shaped a lot of my journey through life... But I had to consciously look at taking what I had learnt and use that to shape me positively. For instance, for a long time I would get stuck thinking, "Why did this happen to me?" This would leave me feeling sorry for myself and would affect how I viewed relationships when I got older. What I learnt is that we need to choose to live a life 'in spite of' these circumstances, instead of deciding to live a life 'because of' them.

Key takeaways

It starts by accepting that both bad and good things happen to everyone and just because you have a good record, doesn't mean that only good things happen to you. Of course, we shouldn't use that excuse to cause chaos and make bad decisions either, because what good does that do?

For whatever your life event has been – that may have or has thrown you off course - we shouldn't "lose hope in the end of the story." Just because life happened doesn't mean that there are no longer positive aspects to look forward to or a reason that may arise from these events that are indeed positive. We can create a new narrative and create a good life for ourselves, despite what may have happened.

It is imperative that we reach a point of acceptance – denial is not a strategy. Even though this may take some time, it is important to realise that what happened, happened, and we need to move on. Living a life always surrounded by negative circumstances, thoughts, and emotions does us no good in the end.

I have also learnt that something may have happened to us so early on in life that we may not fully understand the dynamics, and that there were people close to us responsible for these extraneous circumstances. For example, I have never really grasped the events that shaped my parents' divorce and yes, it took some time to accept, but it took longer to reach a point of forgiveness and understanding that those were the decisions of my parents. I then had to learn to form new relationships with people within the new family dynamic - my parents, my extended family, and my new blended family. Despite the decision made by the people around me, I realised that forming my own individual relationships with people is a better strategy. This is instead of others dictating how I should relate to people.

Why this is important is because then you, as the individual, treat and relate to people based on your own value system and this will be from an authentic place. Should you wish to cut ties with people, that must be your decision. Should you wish to make a relationship work, that should be yours too. For me, I have decided to love despite what happened. I have decided to be open, communicable, loving to all, and to share my life (and my mind – yes my thoughts and opinions are valid and I do have a voice!) with those who are willing to walk that journey with me. Trust me, there is just less drama that way!

A reason why choosing a path of love is more gracious, rather than one of holding grudges, is because I realised that people around us can only give what they are capable of. Living a life stating that, "I wish my parents were more like this at the time", or, "I wish my family helped me with this", only fuels resentment because it carries the weight of our expectations. Realising that life also happened to them and they could only give what they had at that time, allows one to meet people where they are at. We may not agree with people's decisions but we should look through this lens of meeting people where they are at if we wish to carry on and work on the relationships with those who may have caused us pain. I hope you will find the courage to determine your own relationships in this interesting circle of life – no matter what happened. These relationships can be good, bad, or ugly… It's your choice.

GOING AGAINST THE TIDE

THE ROLE YOUR ENVIRONMENT PLAYS

*"The first step toward success is taken when
you refuse to be a captive of the environment
in which you first find yourself."*
—Mark Caine

Point of departure

I have had several debates with Grant, my
partner, about willpower vs environment. The
question we have wrestled with is whether over
time, one's behaviour, choices, thinking patterns,
etcetera are influenced greatly by one's environment, or whether willpower can be the overcomer
of all. Meaning that despite the environment we
find ourselves in, can our willpower steer us in
the right direction? Worth debating about right?

Well, to his point I believe that there is
definitely an argument for willpower. If you
know who you are and can make decisions inde-

pendent of your environment, then you have chosen to live despite your environment, and kudos to you. My counter-argument, however, is that yes, we can all have the willpower we need to survive a certain circumstance, for however long we need to endure, but how come we all want to (secretly, or not) leave a bad or toxic environment? Despite how strong our willpower is to overcome, in our gut, something is saying it's time to go. Further to that argument is that willpower is also like a muscle; it gets stronger, and sometimes it gets weaker. For me, I would rather remove myself from a risky environment in the first place and then continuously strengthen my willpower.

This to me, therefore, concludes that our environment plays a major role in terms of influencing us and can be a cause of contention, creating a disconnect. For a lot of people, a toxic environment can cause them to lose sight of who they really are because what ends up happening is people move into survival mode. From my perspective, it is difficult to thrive when we are merely surviving.

So what environments am I speaking about? This can be your work environment, the situation at home, the environment around extended family or drama-prone friends, as well as your school or church environments, for example.

A leaf from my life

On my life path, I have experienced interesting work environments, where the carrot and stick approach has been used, for instance. This did not enable growth which went against my values. I have been in work environments where gossip is the cup of tea and that soured my whole experience with social circles at work. Furthermore, I have found myself in settings where politicking is the name of the game and I realised why I struggled to trust and why I was always stressed in that environment.

I realised, after doing a detailed personality test that I am not one to play the politics game. It's not my thing and is not in tune with my energy. What was suggested to me is that despite not wanting to play the game, it is important to understand that it is there. Wherever people are gathered, even within a family dynamic, there is politics at play. I came to learn that for me, the best way to navigate such environments is to notice the game and fly under the radar. Let people do their thing and I will do mine. If that works for you, there's a tip to take home.

I remember that gossip and useless banter took place during the years of my parent's divorce and that bred a toxic environment. Even at the age of nine, I could notice and sense it, and for me, it was liberating to leave that environment.

Another thing that can influence us and our value system, and eventual purpose in life, is the schools we attend. I was privileged to attend a school that celebrated diversity and artistic creation while in Uganda. That's why I believed I could become a great creative writer someday. Writing for the school newspaper and getting commendations from some of the most popular kids in school was a real pat on my back. I felt I could be who I was at that place. When I moved schools, very reluctantly, my new school only allowed for a partial creative expression; there were no drama or music classes that one could major in. The only place I felt I could develop creatively was in English, but it wasn't enough for one willing to nurture their creativity.

The culture of the school too, I found to be a little limiting. I came from a place where being who you are was celebrated and rules around what you wore or how you styled your hair weren't so much an issue. I gathered that despite all the rigid rules that most traditional schools implemented, one could still learn well and perform. I'm sure you're sensing my lack of conformity again. In my new school in South Africa, you had to dress a certain way, wear your hair in a particular fashion and I wondered why, and if that would improve my learning capabilities. You may have your point of view, which is fine, but for me, it was limiting and made school life a lot less fun. I believe if kids are taught the right values and have the right principles and disciplines in place - which should ideally come from the home environment - they should be allowed to express themselves, and they should be allowed to be who they are. Also, it's a learning process; we can't know who we are if we are not allowed to express ourselves. So wearing my hair in a particular fashion will not make me more or less capable of learning; just saying!

Point to ponder

Are you in an environment or about to enter one that may not be conducive to your journey in life?

Write out your reflections:

Driving the point home

We all find ourselves in unwanted environments at times. Being aware of our surroundings and what we can do about them is important. Reflecting on our situations is essential. For how long have you been in a disabling environment? Is there an opportunity to change it? Are you able to choose a new environment instead?

Despite how much willpower we have, it is important to understand the environment we've immersed ourselves into as that will determine how we grow and how we learn to trust, all of which will influence many aspects of our lives. Most importantly, environments will shape how we think.

Key takeaways

I have learnt to seek out positive environments where like-minded people help each other grow in various aspects of life. I implore you to seek out environments with people that you can grow with spiritually; who will keep you accountable from a health perspective; that can teach you how to make better financial decisions and create wealth; and that can teach you how to grow into a better version of you. It is unlikely that these things will magically transpire from your mind because if they could, they would have already. We need to get into positive environments or bring them to us in the form of books, audios and podcasts, and we need to associate with them regularly. Have the discipline to regularly associate with such environments as that will also strengthen your willpower.

You can also question your current environment in an attempt to improve it, should you not be able to leave it for whatever reason. Still, the responsibility starts with you to change it. It is, however, difficult to control what others do, should they not be willing to adapt to a better environment. Alternatively you can make the choice to leave it, and find a more suitable one or start a more inclusive one elsewhere.

THE SECRET LIFE OF WORDS[3]

WHAT PEOPLE TELL YOU ABOUT YOURSELF – THEIR UNINTENDED GIFTS

"Words are things. You must be careful… Some day we'll be able to measure the power of words. I think they are things. They get on the walls. They get in your wallpaper. They get in your rugs, in your upholstery, and your clothes, and finally in to you."
—Maya Angelou

Point of departure

Words have a particular impact on us, and they can cause us to question our identity, value system, and worth.

A leaf from my life

Growing up, one thing I used to hear a lot was, "Anna, you're so shy!" I think what people may have been going for was that I was introverted. Shy is not how I would describe myself. As an introverted child, I loved to listen and watch what was going on around me and form narratives in my mind as to how best I understood what was taking place. It was entertaining, and it still is. However, the fact that I heard people mention to each other that I was shy, led to me somehow starting to believe that my introverted nature was actually 'shy'. I took on something that was not me, because I thought, "Hey, these grown-ups know better right?" Little did I know that I had picked up one of life's unintended gifts - people's opinion of you. My 'shyness' began to play an extensive part in my life, where I would find myself withdrawing from certain aspects, not speaking up when I wanted to, and not going out to find new friends or opportunities to work on my creativity.

In that time too, the old saying that children were not to be heard and only seen still applied. An insane idealogy, I agree, but even so, there were no positive connotations attached to being shy then either. Well, what all this meant for an introverted (dubbed 'shy') girl was that it would take me a long time to find my voice.

Point to ponder

What about you? Have you ever adopted a trait others bestowed on you, mistakenly or not, that begins to distort your version of who you are? Are you still personifying that trait?

Write out your reflections:

....

....

....

....

....

....

....

....

....

....

....

....

....

....

....

....

....

....

....

....

....

....

....

....

....

....

....

....

....

....

....

....

....

Driving the point home

People's opinions are very expensive. One should be careful of unsolicited advice too. Remember people will remark on things based on their lens/perspective of life. So be careful whose words you accept and take advice from, and be conscious of the context. Some people have an agenda. Those with our best interests at heart are rare and we must develop the discernment to assess the difference.

What I learnt having listened to an audio titled, "My Computer" by Shad Helmstetter, is that your brain acts like a floppy disk. Everything that you take in is stored in there, like someone capturing data and inputting it into your personal computer hard drive. Whether you realise it or not, the data is stored there and mostly it's in the subconscious. Life's unintended gifts influence us greatly because if we choose to accept them they become part of our DNA, and because they are ingrained in our subconscious we make choices based on them and live life according to their essence.

Key takeaways

How did I realise that I was not shy, but introverted? How did I realise the power I had with my introversion and that it was not a quality beneath someone who was more bubbly and extroverted? I started reading personal development books and did one personality test that changed my perspective completely. After reading the book *Personality Plus*[4], I realised that my personality type was *melancholy choleric*; dominant in the first trait (melancholic), and the latter my next dominant trait. This means that I am very analytical, a planner, but can sometimes be pessimistic while my choleric trait means I am able to take control, lead, and never enjoy being told what to do. That only scratches the surface, and I would encourage you to read and figure out your personality type too.

One of the most important lessons is knowing how you relate with people, and how they relate to you and others. Then you'll figure out why some people seem to always irritate you or want to be the centre of attention; it's not that they want to do that intentionally, it's just who they are.

Another leaf from my life

Another unintended gift I received was about the path I wanted to take as a writer. When I was brave enough to say to people that my dream was writing, I heard a quick passing comment that writing may not be a sustainable career path. Of course, at that time I was not mature enough to understand that this just meant finding a solution to its sustainability because of course, it is seasonal trade. At that time, it stopped me in my tracks to consider whether this was a worthwhile path to take as it reinforced my uncertainty - the uncertainty that originally stemmed from whether taking a path no one I knew had taken before would lead to success. It's funny how the one negative thing someone says gets burned into our memory and regardless of how many other positive statements we receive, it's so difficult to erase that negative memory.

Through the years, I did have positive reinforcements that my writing was good and should be nurtured - from all my English teachers in high school actually. I remember in Grade 8/9 writing a story for an assignment where my

English teacher actually sat up at night to read it, and even lit candles to finish my story when her power went out. Biggest affirmation ever! My English Literature teacher too inspired me to learn more and it was the class I always eagerly awaited. Then in South Africa, working through literature works like Shakespeare and film study was a highlight. It never felt like work. So the experts knew what they were saying and nurturing that talent is something I will keep working on.

Point to ponder

What about you? Are you in a specific field that you really wanted or did other people's unintended gifts sway you from that path? Do you want to get back on that path?

Write out your reflections:

....

....

....

....

....

Key takeaways

You're probably wondering whether I am living the writing dream right now. Well, the truth is that I am working on getting to that path. This book is a great start. I started small, doing literature courses after work and visualising this writing dream, despite all the distractions. So I may not have it all figured out, but I have started. As the *Principle of the Path*, well-articulated by Andy Stanley, states, "You may not be able to change your destination today but you can change direction today."[5] You have to take action and change direction - intention won't get you there. And remember, it's not too late to change direction. You have a dream within you for a specific reason.

Another key lesson I've learnt to handle these unintended gifts is firstly, not to give too much meaning to what everyone says, especially if it causes you to question who you are or what you want to do with your life. The reality is that no one made them the expert of your life.

What may also help to handle these situations is not to take offence. People may offend you by what they say about you or your intentions but you don't have to take it – don't give people that power. Lastly, understand that most people mean well, however, everyone speaks from their perspective; it is okay if those don't align with yours.

PEOPLE LIKE THESE[6]

THE INFLUENCE OF THE PEOPLE
YOU HANG OUT WITH

*"You are the average of the five people you spend
the most time with."*
—Jim Rohn

Point of departure

This one pretty much goes without saying - or so
you would think. What this topic brings to mind
is reading Sean Covey's book, *The 7 Habits of
Highly Effective Teens*, when I was about 14 years
or so, and thinking to myself, "OMG I'm so glad
I learnt this from a book instead of life!" Even
after reading the book, I can't claim that I escaped
the lessons of life though. The people we
surround ourselves with will influence us greatly
and often it takes place unconsciously. In some
interesting way, we end up resembling the

people we interact with constantly; mannerisms, language, ideas, and even the way we think. In my adult years, it was put more tangibly to me: You will earn the average of your five closest friends. That can be a hard one to swallow for some.

A leaf from my life

Even though I was introverted as a young child and teenager, I did hang out with people. I mean, I wasn't a loner. However, I was immediately drawn to some and not to others, because I had this antenna that guided me.

If you would like a deep dive into the influence that personal relationships have on us, Skip Ross' *Dynamic Living Series* audios exemplify this fact even more. He shares a story of a time he and his wife had chosen to live their lives a certain way which meant leaving their closest friends behind. It became impossible for their new chosen path and their old path to coincide, and seeing as their closest friends did not want to change, they had to sit them down and explain that they could either journey with them on this new and better path or they would have to be left behind.

Point to ponder

Have you ever had to make a choice like that? To choose to reduce the amount of time you hang out with certain people you've been around for so long to chase your dream or because your paths no longer align?

Write out your reflections:

....

....

....

....

....

....

....

....

....

....

....

....

....

....

....

....

....

....

....

....

....

....

....

....

....

....

....

....

....

....

....

....

....

....

....

Driving the point home

Who have these people been for you, if at all? I'm not talking about being prideful and abandoning friendships. There are some people that we do have to cut off completely, and graciously, if possible. For others, it may be just about prioritising our time with them. That's more or less what I did when I decided to pursue some goals. Yes, I loved having a social life and hanging out with people but at some point, I had to plan my time better as I couldn't be in two places at once.

The people surrounding you will influence who you are, how you think, and eventually if you give them the power, who you will become. That is something to be mindful of. It is not easy to decide whether or not to change or improve our social circles, or moderate the time spent with certain people. It is, however, necessary to determine the type of characters you want around you to ensure you are keeping with your values and that they will not negatively impact how you think or where you want to go in life.

Key takeaways

What I've ascertained to be able to discern the amount of time I spend with certain people is first, whether they are walking a similar journey as me in a certain aspect of life, and if they have similar value systems. That is usually a good signal for positive influencers you want around. Granted, we all do things differently but this similarity allows for relevant discussions that move both parties forward.

Secondly, asking yourself questions can provide a clear response such as, "Will these people pull me back or propel me further?" Sometimes this question is a difficult one to unpack, but genuinely speaking, and beyond the gut feel, if you know who you are, what your values are, and what you are chasing, you can answer that. Then, finally, you need to act and be able to handle the aftermath, however uncomfortable it may be. You need make a choice, to either change your circle, improve your circle or leave it. If the latter, then you can always find your tribe on the journey towards you.

10 THINGS I LOVE
ABOUT YOU[7]

*"Become the person the person you're looking
for is looking for."*
—Andy Stanley

Point of departure

The person you date, choose as a life partner, or
marry, will have a significant influence on you
in terms of either derailing you from your
authentic self and your true purpose, or they can
help in propelling you further and towards it.

A leaf from my life

I was very fortunate to meet Grant when I met
him. He embodies something I did not see a lot
in other guys – his willingness to grow and to

grow together. From the moment I met him and the level of deep discussions we had, it was obvious I was going to enjoy talking to him endlessly and that we would constantly challenge each other to ensure we become the best version of ourselves.

As an aside, if you're familiar with the principle of attraction, I believe I attracted Grant into my life in some way. I remember reading the book, *The Secret*, based on the 'Law of Attraction', which highlighted that you can attract anything you want. So dutifully, I sat down and wrote all the characteristics I would want to find in my lifelong partner and labelled it *Mr. Man*. You may think it's simple, or from a naïve perspective or really cute, but the point is I wrote it down. I then had a template for what I wanted and it was clear how to discern the princes from the frogs. When I met Grant some years later (approximately four years later) and we had been dating for a little while, I brought the page up from my laptop and we went through it together… talk about being vulnerable! Would you believe it if I told you that he generally ticked every single box except three or so out-of-the-box items I added? Look, I don't mean to promote a tick-box exercise but rather to promote the importance of knowing what you want so that when it's around, you grab it with open arms.

Anna and Grant four years after they met

Our relationship did not come without its challenges, of course. For instance, we both have very strong characteristics, which clashed at times; so doing personality tests allowed us to understand each other better. We also came from two different cultures, backgrounds, and religious/spiritual upbringings and we had to come to terms with that, and decide how we would want to move forward together. What is formidable has been the level of communication to be able to navigate some interesting and challenging conversations. It comes down to good communication in the end… as cliché as that sounds.

The topic of dreams and goals, and how we can support each other continues to be at the forefront of our discussions as that is very important to keep us in tune with what the other is pursuing. I know it sounds a bit like a fairy tale, but yeah, what can I say? In as smooth as I'm making our relationship sound, it was not always like that. We had - and will have - interesting bumps along the way, but we believe we have built a strong foundation by putting the work into our relationship; something we will continue to do.

What has also been to our advantage, is knowing that to attract the person we wanted to be with, we would first have to become the best version of ourselves. As Andy Stanley puts it, you want to "become the person the person you're looking for is looking for."[8] Before we even met, personal development was on top of both of our agendas, and it has consistently been a part of our relationship.

We both had interesting and rocky paths to navigate, and baggage from the past as everyone does, but we put in the time to read books and understand how best to navigate into a growth-filled relationship. The key is we were preparing, even before we met, we prepared during our initial dating years, and continue to do so as we walk this journey together.

Point to ponder

Is the person you've decided to walk alongside in life someone who is propelling you further or holding you back? Perhaps it's time to have a candid discussion with yourself and each other to see how to remedy the situation.

Write out your reflections:

....

....

....

....

Driving the point home

Again, awareness is key and there is room for communication with each other. In what aspect would you say your partner is influencing you either positively or negatively? Have you affirmed their positive impacts? Perhaps you are holding back your significant other? What can you do to remedy the situation?

Remember what we mentioned about willpower vs environment. Should you find yourself in the company of someone who does not have the best interests at heart for you and your life, it will be very difficult to have a genuinely happy relationship and life. Remember, you are both walking through life alongside each other. Yes, you may have different dreams and goals internally (and what you bring into the relationship) but if you look at what you are building together, your dreams and goals will begin to align.

Key takeaways

Preparing for relationships and marriage is essential; it is not fluff. There is a variety of information out there to help us prepare in this regard. I look at how so many people jump into relationships and marriage with no preparation but expecting success. Imagine that most of us spend seven years or so studying towards a particular qualification but when it comes to a choice that should last a lifetime, we don't put in the same amount of effort. Riding on the emotions of love as a viable strategy to help you navigate life with your chosen person is not adequate. Those initial emotions eventually fade out but in order to keep them alive, we all need to learn useful skills in that area continuously.

I would recommend delving into some books first, such as *Love and Respect*[9]. Gary Chapman also has a range of books in this area regarding the *Five Love Languages*[10] to *Things I Wish I'd Known Before We Got Married*[11]. Another interactive book to consider that you and your partner can work through together is the *101 Questions to Ask Before You Get Engaged.*[12] There are also several podcasts and channels to engage in this aspect too. Some channels that have made a significant difference to Grant and me, in terms of practical teachings, are Andy Stanley's series on relationships. These include, *What Happy*

Couples Know,[13] and to demystify the myths on dating and relationships, check out his series *The New Rules for Love, Sex and Dating.*[14] Thereafter, find a couples/marriage course that is suitable for both of you and talk to couples you trust for some practical hands-on perspectives.

It is imperative to keep reading and engaging with such material throughout one's relationship. Doing the work at the front-end while expecting long-lasting results is also not the solution. We must keep learning and growing in this area because as individuals and couples, we are also growing and changing and different points in the journey together will require some new skills or a refresher. So please prepare.

THE ART OF YES AND NO

THE IMPACT OF THE CHOICES YOU MAKE

"It doesn't matter which side of the fence you get off on sometimes. What matters most is getting off. You cannot make progress without making decisions."
—Jim Rohn

Point of departure

The choices we make are an integral part of who we are, who we become, and how our lives eventually turn out to be. Making choices is an important life skill.

As we get older, we learn to make our own choices, be it who we want to be, what we want to study, what career we want to venture into, or who to date and marry - you catch my drift. I have come across several people, myself included, who have stumbled many times because of being unable to make certain decisions. I have realised that sometimes indecisiveness doesn't only arise because we don't know what we want; I think it stems from an even deeper point of us losing sight of who we are, and so the choices we have in front of us (and eventually make) are not our own but from other sources of influence. Then, as we go through life, we keep making choices based on other people's or society's influences until we do not know why we are making certain decisions after all!

A leaf from my life

For a while, I have battled with the decision between getting a Master's in the field I'm working in or in an entirely new area, or not at all. Before you jump in with your version of the answer, please understand I may not see things from your point of view. It's been a constant question that I've been grappling with for a year or so now and quite frankly, I am still yet to solve the problem. I read an article on decision theory which suggests that sometimes a pros and cons analysis of a problem doesn't always yield the answer. So yes I've made the pros and cons list and I've even gone as far as applying overseas and being accepted into two really great schools.

However, there is still that unnerving feeling in my gut suggesting that I'm not sure if it's what I really want to do.

You see, some would just say, do it, there is so much time in life, or one needs to get ahead and you can't without this paper. Well, they are right but they are also thinking linearly in terms of believing that it is the only way to be successful. In my mind, there are more things to consider than just the qualifications. I'm still on the fence about it because if I were to do a Master's in my field, I need to be sure I want to continue working in my field or to do something with it. If I were to do one in an entirely different field, I would need to make it work and find a new career path too. If I decide not to do it at all, I would have to ensure I develop in an entirely different direction. So the reason for grappling is to ensure I choose based on what I really want to achieve in life, and not just for the sake of doing it or because someone else suggests it; because then that's on someone else's account.

Why I have come to this realisation is because for a long time I have been making choices in my life that would ensure my survival. For example, studying for a particular degree, which may not have been my first choice, to get a job so I could be financially secure. Even though doing Economics was interesting - and I have made the decision right by looking for areas I enjoy in that field and applying it there - I would say it's my second love, not my first.

I think for me, based on what happened in my past I have not ventured onto a path that may be my first love because firstly, I didn't get an opportunity to nurture it to see how I can create a career out of it. Writing, while growing up, was portrayed as something that was not really serious and could leave one financially vulnerable. The last thing I wanted was not to be able to survive. But I am wiser now, and life has taught me that there are various ways to make money and pursue one's purpose as well. So once I've got an answer to this internal journey I will get back to you.

Point to ponder

Are you about to make a certain choice that may not be your own choice but is based on other people's idea of how-things-should-be?

Write out your reflections:

....

....

....

....

....

....

....

....

....

....

....

....

....

....

....

....

....

....

Driving the point home

The choices we make will impact and continue to influence who we are because we have to live with those choices and embed them into our lives. For example, if we choose to study a particular course, we will most likely end up in a similar career and that shapes a trajectory. Granted, careers can be altered at some point, but the amount of time spent learning a particular trade will very likely shape how you process things, see the world, your interests, and prospects thereafter. So being mindful of the choices we make for ourselves and of their related consequences is worth considering.

Key takeaways

So, you may be a lot better at making decisions than me, because for a while, making decisions often got me into a frenzy and I would freeze. I suffered a lot from decision fatigue and indecisiveness. What I have learnt is that making decisions is like a muscle. We need to practice and exercise that muscle. No one is born with decision-making skills; we have to develop them. So if you relate, perhaps it's time to start practising how to make decisions.

I have also learnt that it's okay to change your mind. Once you realise the decision you have to make is not based on your authentic path, it is okay to change your mind. Don't beat yourself up for the way you were thinking before. It's also important to realise that sometimes we won't always make the right choices, but we will learn to make better ones, especially if we exercise that muscle. We all have an opportunity to do that.

Lastly, I've also discovered that we also have an opportunity to make our choices right. This means that once we've decided on something, we must make it the best possible opportunity. There is a lot more that follows after the choice is made, and we want to make sure we get the best out of it, so follow through with action steps that make your choice the right one.

GREAT EXPECTATIONS[15]

"I cannot give you the formula for success, but I can give you the formula for failure. It is: Try to please everybody."
—Herbert Bayard Swope

Point of departure

This section stems directly from the choices we make; being that if we have already made choices that were not really our own, and we are living certain aspects of our life because of those choices, where do we go from there?

A leaf from my life

I'm sure you've heard so many people who've said that they only studied a particular subject at university because that is what their family or parents wanted them to do or expected them to do. Or taking it a notch deeper, some would say they could only date/marry this particular person, from this particular background, with this particular religious upbringing, because that is what was expected from where they came from.

It is well known that some parents want to live their lives through their children like it's their second attempt at life. Unfortunately, their influences and desires will impact their children, causing children to lose sight of what they want. Of course, most of them mean well and want the best for their kids, but there is a fine line where parents' hopes and dreams for their kids should not overtake their kids' own personal desires and choices. And if it does, children should be able to speak up and ask parents/caregivers the question, "Why?" Communication should assist in enabling people to be on the same page and this will help us make more authentic choices going forward.

For example, for me, I've often wondered whether I should continue doing the things I was brought up doing, even when I don't fully understand them, or forge my own path. One instance is my religious upbringing. I am very grateful for it and the values that it instilled in me, but now I want to understand a lot more about it and ask the questions that I am still uncertain about. I am now working on figuring out aspects of religion, Christianity, and spirituality for myself.

Also, as a lighter example, growing up I always thought one had to do strenuous exercises (running and gym galore) to stay fit and healthy. When I started my health and wellness business I quickly realised that that wasn't the case. We can do a lot more harm to our bodies than good with strenuous exercise. Moderate exercise like walking is even more efficient in the weight-loss process, for example. Now, long walks, Pilates, and some Zumba-strong have become my go-to workouts. My point is that we should do intelligent due diligence, without pride, and be open to learning and then we pick what works for us and our value system. We don't always have to do what so and so did, and what so and so before them did.

Point to ponder

Would you say you have made certain choices that were not really your own but were based on other people's idea of how-things-should-be?

Write out your reflections:

....

....

....

....

....

....

....

....

....

....

....

....

....

....

I'm sure we have all done so. I certainly have. Now the question we must answer is what to do about that realisation. We need to reflect and ask ourselves a few questions: Why did we make that decision? How did we conclude that certain decision? Who was involved in that decision? When did it occur? What was the decision? We can change our decision if that is possible, but more importantly, going forward we must ask ourselves whether the choice is truly ours or not. We need to self-reflect and ask ourselves these questions. Sometimes we may also need to ask others as to why there is a certain expectation for us to do something or be someone.

Driving the point home

I will end off with a famous story to illustrate this point further - the story of the oven. Forgive me if it is not word for word but it emphasises the point in a relatable fashion.

A mother and daughter were making turkey/chicken one night and before placing it in the oven, the mother cut off both ends of the chicken and tossed them away. Upon watching this from a distance, her daughter asked, "Why are you cutting off the ends of the chicken?" To which the mother replied, "I don't know, my mother always used to do the same thing." The daughter stated, "Perhaps we should call grandmother and ask her why." The mother agreed and considered calling her mom to inquire. The grandmother, pleased to hear from them but surprised at the question, responded to say, "Well, honey I don't know - my mother also used to do the same thing!" Unsatisfied with the answer the little girl suggested they call her great grandmother. The mother proceeded to ask her grandmother the same question. Surprised by the call, great grandmother laughed and replied, "Well dear, I cut off the ends of the chicken because, in those days, the oven was too small!"

So, are we doing things/living life based on a trend, or based on what other people in the past did? If so, and we understand why, then great. If we do not understand why and are perpetuating past or current traits, we need to ask the question, "Why?" This is because this sort of mindset will also influence our future choices. We can make decisions based on what's been done in the past, or what's acceptable to those around us, or we can do our research and make our own authentic choices.

Key takeaways

It is important to reflect and figure out whether we have been doing this in our lives. Do we spend money as everyone else does? Do we work as everyone else does? Do we have to keep up with appearances because that's what's expected? Do we perpetuate patriarchy because that's what's culturally been practised? Well, it takes a good look in the mirror to consider these aspects and to be honest with ourselves.

Should we find we have been living a life based on other people's or society's expectations, then where can one go from there? Well, the way I see it, we can either continue on the same path but realise that nothing new or positive may come from it, or we can change our direction and start living based on our value systems.

Granted, there are certain life-long consequences that come as a result of the choices we have made that may not be as easy to change. We need to acknowledge the part we played in these long-lasting choices and going forward we must self-reflect and make better decisions. Remember, you may not be able to change circumstances overnight but you can certainly change direction. So, decide to make choices based on your value system so you can live your authentic story. It will be the most unique one out there!

HIDDEN FIGURES[16]

"No one can make you feel inferior without your consent."
—**Eleanor Roosevelt**

Point of departure

How you view yourself and what you say to yourself (that little voice in your head) is an integral part of determining how you live out your life. If there is any inconsistency between who you believe you truly are and the way you see yourself currently, or how you talk to yourself, then there is something worth changing. Otherwise, we become the version we create in our heads, and sometimes that can be very limiting and most likely based on external influences... Remember when we talked about the 'unintended gifts' from other people?

A leaf from my life

Growing up, there was an area that I had to define as it constantly seemed misplaced to me. I remember being told that I was such a tomboy when I was younger. Well, if you think about it, there are many reasons behind that. Firstly, I grew up around many boys - my brothers - and did not really grow up with my mum to have influenced me otherwise. The truth is I loved dungarees (for those of you who still remember those)! They were comfortable and easy-going. After some time, I was quickly initiated to dresses, high-heeled pink slippers (those were gorgeous), and other such things. This started me on a journey where I learnt to love pretty things, which was great. However, it made me wonder whether there was something out of place in me because these girly items were not my immediate go-to items.

I can recall a few experiences that were embarrassing and kicked my self-esteem and belief in myself. I got invited to a friend's sweet 16, and the party dress code was formal. Look, there was no Google or Pinterest or anyone to ask at that time, so I rocked up in my favourite pastel pink pants and a really lovely white bedazzled top. Well, despite the bedazzling, I was severely underdressed and was called out in front of everyone. Looking back, I think it was more their lack of maturity than my dress code that wasn't on. Anyway, it started making me believe that I had no idea how to dress or operate in social circles.

Something similar also took place when I saw my friends in high school putting on mascara and I was like, "Oh, so is that the one you put on your eyelashes and the eye pencil at the bottom?" I think they were more shocked than embarrassed for me and gave me a gentle laugh. Look, I was curious and eager to learn because the self-belief that was building was a negative thought that I wasn't good at any of these lady-like things.

I also used to get comments about my skin because it was just covered in spots, only to add to the pressure that I didn't have anyone to really teach me how to take care of it or that I was just not good at these lady-like things...

Well, that self-belief perpetuated for a while and it resulted in much lower self-esteem about my appearance, though these feelings didn't feel right internally. I'm getting to the point. What the outcome of this was, was that inside I felt and still acted very confidently but when it came to matters of appearance, I was not winning the war inside my head.

Point to ponder

Has a situation in life (or occurrences of them) made you have a different belief about yourself, compared to what you actually feel inside? Has there been a disconnect between your self-belief and who you truly are, or at least feel that you are?

Write out your reflections:

....

....

....

....

....

....

....

....

....

....

Driving the point home

It is no secret that we have questioned ourselves in the past. What are you repeating to yourself? Are these mainly positive or negative thoughts? We need to be careful and capture these negative thoughts so they do not cement themselves in us. Being aware of why, and how often they occur, allows us to manage them.

What you tell yourself will continue to perpetuate. Whether that self-belief emanated from your head (hidden figures within) or from other people, you may want to change the narrative to work in your favour. Change the narrative so that there is unity between who you are internally and how you show up in life.

Key takeaways

What I did to change my narrative was to take action. I got to a point where I was old enough to make the decisions about what I wore and could start purchasing things for myself. So, I developed my style and figured out what fashion I liked and what I didn't. It took some streamlining but I got there. I like to think of my style as one that finds the most unique items out there (whenever I can) and blends them to suit me. For example, I recently found a personal designer who made my matric dance dress and my 30th birthday outfit, which I designed! Who knew I had a skill for that. There you go… narrative changed.

I also went on a journey to fix my skincare because that was not working for my self-esteem. I appreciate all the help I had along the way, where people bought products for me and my aunts even taught me how to do the three-step process (Cleanse – Tone – Moisturise, i.e. CTM). I think my skincare journey and my marketing business were meant to intersect because that is when I found a solution for myself. When I started in my business, I looked to develop as a skincare consultant where I discovered a prestige brand to work with. I used it for six months for myself and have never looked back. It was so great having a community of people who taught me and engaged with me on everything about the brand because it was life-saving - literally. I am now able to give people the gift I never had. I can teach people about skincare and the benefits of looking after it. To the point that all my siblings use the same skincare brand as me, and even my Aunts who taught me the basic CTM many years ago. They looked at my skin and said, "Hey, I need what you have." Well, what can I say? Narrative changed – yet again.

Having discovered what personality type I was (melancholy choleric) I also realised why I enjoyed going on my own journey of discovery. I needed to be in a place that I could get information (which is what a melancholy craves). Therefore, developing my own style and being in a community that taught skincare tactics was much needed.

I also realised that I was not aloof while at social gatherings, it was just that I really enjoyed watching and listening. I have learnt now, that I can still be engaging at social get-togethers, in order to contribute, and so I tap into my inner charm whenever needed.

A quote that still works for me today is to "be mindful of what you say to yourself, and even more mindful of what you say to yourself when you are alone" (unknown).

In whatever area you feel your self-belief is not quite there yet, it is imperative to choose and practice a new paradigm. And also, if an environment is a reason that causes you to doubt yourself, go where you are celebrated and not tolerated. Learn who you are, and why your personality may cause you to go into a certain disposition. It is important to learn your strengths to use them appropriately and to manage your weaknesses. At the end of the day, you don't want to be your own worst enemy. Change your narrative and use it to propel you forward.

FACING GIANTS[17]

FAILURE WHEN YOU TRY SOMETHING

"It's not whether you get knocked down,
it's whether you get up."
—Vince Lombardi

Point of departure

There are things in life we know we want to
pursue, or should already be doing because they
identify with what is true to us. For some people
it is teaching, working in a creative field, baking,
running a business, writing a book, or living a
healthy lifestyle. For most of us, we have
contemplated how to pivot towards what we
want to pursue, and because we cannot see
HOW things should be done, these pursuits live
inside our heads and remain that... purely
wishes. However, some others of us take some

action even if the HOW is not yet clear. For instance, we talk to people in those fields or take a class to discover if that interest is a deep interest or just wishful thinking.

For those of us who take action (and I implore those who haven't to also do so), we quickly realise that we face stumbling blocks along the way. These stumbling blocks can lead us to question our path and the reason we are doing things in the first place. Perhaps it's the free social time we have to sacrifice to work on our pursuit and dreams or it's the negativity we face from often well-meaning people around us - who are really just scared to follow their dreams. Sometimes the stumbling block is a harsh price tag we face if our business does not profit as intended. Perhaps it's the rejection we face from the audition or role we were praying for. What then? What is our next step?

A leaf from my life

Well if you're reading this book then you are pretty much aware of the narrative of failing forward. So I'll continue with that as the benchmark. Yes, we know we must fail forward but honestly, it is so much easier said than done; at least for me.

For me, I have always wanted to write books and I have tried to do so several times, including little short stories here and there and two novels that I almost completed; but somehow they are all stuck in my laptop. So for 10 years, I went down the 'path B of my life' in survivalist mode, convinced that yes I do love writing books but I am no good at completing them, so what would be the point of continuing. However, you and I both know that when there is something we are meant to be doing in life, it will continue to hound us until we make it a reality.

As I started building my marketing business, which has a huge self-development component, I started getting exposed to several personal development books that awakened my writing dream and my dream to communicate with others on matters that would give people a life-changing perspective. I knew I had to get back to my writing. What I realised is I had created excuses for myself over the last decade, and I was just procrastinating on my dream. I had created a belief that came as a result of the procrastination… that I had failed my writing dream. In all honestly, I just had to be brave enough to pick myself up, admit that I was indeed procrastinating, find a way not to procrastinate, and get going with the writing. What's interesting is that the procrastination doesn't just go away and I have had to make an effort to be accountable to myself and others to finish this particular book, for example. As you see, the work doesn't stop and if procrastination is a fault of yours too, face it head-on by taking action.

Another false belief that I had come across was that it would take too long to complete a book. I used to tell myself that I am working, running a business, I've got all these chores… where will I find the time? This is until I came across and attended a course on writing and publishing a book within a year, by the Golden Goose Institute. It taught me that the act of writing just needed to be broken down into a couple of 'sittings' and one measures their progress by the number of words. I realised I could complete a whole book (properly structured) in a much shorter period! So here is where

I find myself, writing and completing the first book that audiences will benefit from. It is a real privilege I tell you ☺

While running my business, I also came across several stumbling blocks which ranged from the lack of belief that I was proficient enough, or that people would not take me seriously. When I didn't hit the goals that I had set out, I knew some were by my own doing due to a lack of action because of the insecurities I had. It would be easy to say business and entrepreneurship is not for me, but that wouldn't be true. I now realise how important entrepreneurship is for me as it has become such a fulfilling part of my life. Being able to serve people and solve problems by applying my creativity is very rewarding.

Something I also ascertained about setting goals in pursuit of my dreams, is that the deadline can always shift, and that is encouraging. Just because I didn't hit the goal at the exact specific time doesn't mean I give up the dream in its entirety. I learnt that the more action I took towards working at my business, the more confident I became and the better I became at reaching certain targets I set for myself. I am sure this will be the same for you, on whichever pursuit you are chasing. The idea is to "set your goals in concrete and your plans in sand" (Jim Dornan).

Point to ponder

Have you ever given up on a dream or goal because you failed to make it materialise when you wanted to? What is holding you back from getting up and moving forward?

Write out your reflections:

....

....

....

....

....

....

....

....

Driving the point home

I heard a great illustration of stumbling blocks to emphasise this point. This illustration I believe comes from the audio by Skip Ross on 'Dynamic Living'. Let's imagine you are driving towards a certain destination, which represents your goal or dream, and at some point, your fuel gauge starts blinking calling for more gas, and subsequently, you stop at a gas station. That gas station is like your stumbling block. Ordinarily, you wouldn't end up stopping there. You would fill up, do what you need to do, and hit the road. Unfortunately, most people's dreams and goals stop at the gas station. Where are your dreams and goals currently? Do you need a jump start or a push out of the gas station?

Key takeaways

A great piece of advice I have come across is that if you need to pause, reflect or mourn something you have failed at, give yourself a short deadline and when the deadline hits, get up and move on. It is not about how many times you fail - that is part of the journey and falling is guaranteed;

what is critical is how quickly you get up and move forward.

The journey of success involves failure, the two cannot exist without each other. We need to accept this fact and then embrace the journey will all its ups and downs so that we do not become emotionally tied only to the successes. Otherwise, we risk being emotional wrecks which is not a very pretty picture.

We also need to be adaptive and pivot to improve on what we learn, as failure is a wonderful teacher. If we do not learn and improve accordingly, we may find ourselves making the same mistakes, and going round in circles.

It is also essential to be someone else's 'hurt locker' where we can. If we have walked the same journey someone else is about to embark on, we can offer them a helping hand and highlight which stepping stones they should walk on and which ones they shouldn't, to soften the learning curve for them. For me, this is a measure of true humility and sometimes we end up having people come along with us on our journey because we have built trust, by assisting them. This will only launch us further. Remember you can "go faster alone but you will go further with people" (African Proverb, paraphrased).

THROUGH THE LOOKING GLASS[18]

THE IMPACT OF UNFULFILLED EXPECTATIONS

"We must look at the lens through [which] we see the world, as well as the world we see, and [understand] that the lens itself shapes how we interpret the world."
—**Stephen R. Covey**

Point of departure

This chapter may sound similar to the former, in that it deals with the expectations we had for something that did not materialise. However, I want to frame this section from a different perspective and let it deal with unfulfilled expectations when it comes to the relationships we have with those around us.

We've already understood that the environment, the people we hang out with and the words people use towards us have a massive impact on us. I wonder if we've taken a second to consider a different angle; that how we see the world and the expectations we have of people do have an impact on us as well.

What do I mean by this? So as an example, when we are younger we probably admire one or two people; for most people, it's your parents or an older sibling. We form a picture of who they are and how they relate to us, and as we go through life, we expect other parents or people to act more or less in the same loving and caring fashion. It could be the opposite where you grow up with difficult relationships and are unable to trust, and therefore you continue to find it difficult to trust even as you associate with people into adulthood, because according to your lens people, in general, are untrustworthy. In whichever instance, you have formed a picture based on your expectations of 'how things should be.' This lens you look through then affects how you conduct yourself and treat those around you.

The problem that may arise that may cause us to reconsider whether our looking glass is accurate, or if we have the right lens, is when our expectations are not reciprocated by others. If you are, for instance, a kind and honest person and you expect those around you to be kind and honest, but they mistreat you and politicise their way through life, what does this mean for you then? Is it easier to adjust and also become mean and dishonest because that may save you the trouble of getting hurt? Or do you keep your benchmark and remain kind and honest but a little wiser, knowing that not everyone else had the benefit of these virtues in their lives?

I have noticed that these expectations we have may be pure and slowly get diluted by how others treat us in life. Sometimes we choose to settle and change who we are to accommodate how others treat us, even though this causes us to disconnect from our true selves.

A leaf from my life

I have seen lots of people change and become overly superficial, make wrong choices because that is what they are experiencing from the relationships around them, or that is what culture dictates. For example, choosing to be meaningful and to have deep conversations with friends, peers, or work colleagues, can often get us shut down by others. "Stop being so smart!" or, "Stop being a know-it-all!" gets shoved in our faces. Culture doesn't like the clean-cut perspectives; it wants *the good, the bad, and the ugly.* After all, that's where all the drama lies. What does one do in such a situation?

For me, I've always worn my emotions on my sleeve. I even cried at a Justin Bieber concert (I'm sure you would have done so too, that was an incredible concert… or maybe not, may have just been me.) I digress… I've always wanted to converse deeply and ask a lot of questions especially when things are not going well or are not clear. However, this has not always been reciprocated for me growing up; whatever the reason, it has left me with a lot of unanswered questions. Looking back, I think everyone was dealing with their situations and there I was demanding answers. I do not regret my curious nature, however, and if you know anything about me, I will ask the questions regardless of how uncomfortable they are. I want to make things clear for everyone around me so others can also make the best decisions for themselves. Anyway, this is how I show up in the world, looking for answers and clarity for me and others.

In the earlier parts of my childhood, through my lens, everyone was kind and loving and shared openly and I took that attribute through into adulthood. In my later young adult years, I realised that not everyone around me was willing to share openly and it took peeling an onion to get any honest information out of people. I often wondered why, and why I couldn't talk about everything important with my parents, for example. I know African cultures like to be hush-hush but what good has that done? What this meant for me was that I pivoted from sharing anything with anyone and avoided asking meaningful questions. It made me put up walls and I stopped being fun-loving and carefree, which felt like I was being a shadow version of myself. I also realised, as I went through life, that other people put up many walls too, so maybe this was an all too common defence strategy.

What I realised and learnt later, is that I had expectations of how family life should be and the relationship I wanted with my parents. These were good and pure expectations and I believe I should have received some honest answers, but it wasn't fair to hold a grudge against them for not fulfiling my expectations. What I learnt in my late twenties is that people can only offer you what they have. They cannot give more than they have internally. If there was room for more open conversations with my family, I'm sure we would have had them. This realisation lifted a weight off my shoulders and thereafter, I was more open to meeting people and my family where they were at and loving them for who they were.

Now, for example, my dad and I have a fun and interesting relationship we have built where we confide in each other on shared interests. As two entrepreneurs we like to share what the other is working on and support each other in that realm. One of my favourite memories is sharing the same hotel building with him, where the lift literally had to go downstairs to go upstairs! We also went to the same gym in that hotel which was cool and did a father-daughter dinner at a revolving restaurant in Nairobi. So as you see, the narrative is changing!

Point to ponder

Are you carrying the weight of expectations of how other people should treat you? Do you show up differently in the world because the expectations you had/ve do not match what you're experiencing in life?

Write out your reflections:

....

....

....

....

....

....

....

....

....

....

....

....

....

....

....

....

....

....

....

....

....

....

....

....

....

....

....

....

....

....

....

....

....

....

....

Driving the point home

What helped me change the narrative I had, you may ask? The idea is to have a positive expectancy always! Rather than carrying the weight of expectations. I came across an interesting illustration of expectations versus expectancy. One definition of expectancy is "the state of thinking or hoping that something, especially something good, will happen."[19] This is more future-thinking and is flexible. Expectations, on the other hand, are built on past experiences and have weight, meaning that they carry disappointment should the intended action not materialise.

If we are expectant that we will have positive relationships with people or that people will treat us respectfully and kindly (despite the past or present circumstance) then our mental state is more open to positive things taking place and will allow room for that. Whether or not other people choose to reciprocate this is not a reflection on us as we have done our bit.

I have also heard the idea that some people choose to have negative expectations so that when things don't materialise, they are not disappointed. I would argue that the mental state in this regard does not exactly help in attracting positive things into our lives. Going to a business pitch thinking your prospect will say no, is not a great strategy. Or proposing to the love of your life thinking they will say no… you catch my drift. Because then one would argue, why take any action at all if a negative mental state is what you're after? I would pivot to say that we should have high positive expectancy rather than expectations. Hopefully, this works for the latter group of thinkers too.

Key takeaways

For me, I have an expectancy that my relationships will be of deep quality and I am attracting people around me who appreciate that too. So, in summary, here are a couple of light examples that illustrate the point further and offer some take-home ideas.

Let's say your friends all threw you a birthday party one year, we can't expect them to throw one all the time and we should not treat them otherwise because they don't. It's wise to have a positive expectancy that they will do something great for your birthday, whatever it is and however simple, but we can't tie having expectations to having a party like the one you had last year.

If your work colleagues for example are politicising everything and making your work life impossible, I'm not sure becoming a back-stabber is the right approach. We need to be wise and fly under the radar if possible but changing who we are to fit it in, may not work out in the long term for us.

If you're the type who would spend a weekend helping a friend out but you feel that isn't being reciprocated by others around you, it may not mean you should stop being there for other people if that is truly who you are. Perhaps figure out if you have expectations of others and if you would like it reciprocated. Do communicate it; people may surprise you. And if they are unable to come to your aid in the same fashion that you do it, remember people can only offer what they have.

It's important to understand the expectations we set and understand where they come from. If they need altering or reframing, we should do so. Communicate to someone close to see whether you are viewing things from the lens of expectations.

This is in no way advocating for settling for less, however, because if we are expectant then I believe we are not settling. We should not stop being who we are because it may not be reciprocated by others. I would argue that changing who we are to suit culture, is settling.

WAKE UP AND DREAM[20]

NOT HAVING A PLAN

"If you set goals and go after them with all the determination you can muster, your gifts will take you places that will amaze you."
—Les Brown

Point of departure

If time stopped and you were the only one in existence, who would you be? What would you do?

The path of self-discovery is not an easy one. Some people take action towards learning about themselves and what they truly want from life. Others allow circumstances to determine that for them; I'll call that a laissez-faire approach.

When we know who we are, we have a better idea of what we want from life. It is important not to always concern ourselves with what we want to do, as being busy has become such an obsession. It is vitally important to concern ourselves with who we want to be.

We have discussed in great length about things that may influence who you are and who you become and things that may prevent you from being who you really are. So at the end of it, I hope that the steps we have taken together in this book can help you realise who you are, and then help you decide who you want to be. Do you want to be kinder, more peaceful in your mannerisms, a better parent, a better sibling or friend, more honest or more vulnerable? Do you want to be a better listener, more open, more carefree?

Once we know who we want to be, then we can shape what we want to do. What we do should be in synchronicity with who we are, and we should aim for that as much as possible. This is why I included this chapter. Not having a plan for what we want to do can also cause us a lot of confusion… because at the end of the day we've got to choose what to do and how we spend our time. Let us ensure what we do is something that truly fulfils us.

This topic of mapping out our purposes deserves an entire book on its own. A great book on finding out what we want to achieve in life is Allan and Barbara Pease's book, *The Answer*. I will assume that if you have gotten this far into my book, then you understand the important link between knowing who you are and where you want to go in life.

Not knowing what we want from life, even if it is for a season, leads us to go in circles, which is not ideal. For example, going through life believing that a certain path will lead us to greener pastures is not an effective strategy, if we can look ahead and see that it doesn't. Let me illustrate. If we want to live a life where we are in control of our day, for example, but are working for someone else, we can intend for us to own our day but the reality is that that path is unlikely. It's not the intention that matters, it's the path. We all live, act, and do things in a certain direction as highlighted in *The Principle of the Path*.[21] If you don't like the direction you are heading in life, then change it; because you can change direction immediately and so the destination will be altered for the better in the future. So it's important to know where you want to go and then put your GPS on lock!

I can appreciate that some people want life to be a natural discovery, come as it may. Well, if you know anything about time, it waits for no one. I think it's important to let things take shape but towards the direction we want it to. So this then means we need to take action, make some effort and make decisions as to how we want to live our lives. It's been said often enough that we are where we are right now, because of the decisions we have made. We cannot blame external factors like the economy, our families, our spirituality, etcetera, but only ourselves. Yes, external factors may have shaped our internal processing systems but ultimately we choose how to respond and proceed. Therefore, ultimately we are responsible for how our lives turn out and are responsible for choosing the path that allows us to live a life that is true to us.

So letting things transpire over time (a laissez-faire approach) is not an adequate strategy (in my opinion) towards self-discovery or towards choosing the direction we live our lives. This is because it takes a conscious effort to discover ourselves and to choose a direction, and eventually we will become masters of ourselves if we choose to practice knowing ourselves better, as well as what we want.

A leaf from my life

My first life plan lesson was given to me when I was probably 13. This is the first time I was introduced to the concept of goal setting and life planning. Before that, ignorance ruled and it was blissful to know that my life was in the control of my parents at that stage. When I realised that I could choose what I wanted for my life, it was energising. If you know anything about me, it is that I like to plan and organise. So when someone explained to me that I can map out a 10-year, then 5-year, and a 1-year strategy, my mind was blown! So my 13-year-old brain created a life plan up to the age of 30. I will let you in on a secret: I am 30 now, and looking back at that plan, I am very proud of my younger self and I understand her a bit better.

The first thing I recall when I was writing out this plan at 13 is that there were naturally a lot of gaps. I didn't know what to write because I hadn't been exposed to much. Secondly, the things I wrote resembled what was expected of me and what everyone else around me was largely doing. Anyway, those became much of my guiding principles for a while, and probably till the end of high school, I lived by those principles which is expected but perhaps it wasn't the most open-minded thing to have done.

This is because what I missed to incorporate into my life plan, was allowing for change. I was changing all the time, my interests were growing and I was still finding out who I was and what I wanted to be. However, I didn't know that I should be adapting my life plan constantly, as maturity and discernment became new values I developed later. So I stuck with the goals of wanting to climb the corporate ladder and buying a house by 30, for instance.

What started to happen is that as I got older, subconsciously, these were my measure of success, and when I was nowhere close to reaching them, there was pressure building inside me and I was unaware as to why. Later on, when I started doing proper goal setting, allowing for adaptations and positive expectancy, I then realised the reason for the pressure I felt mounting inside of me.

A great illustration is from a film I watched (I learn a lot from movies as you can tell). This one was about two dancers trying to make a break. As the storyline unfolded, there was another sub-story on following one's dreams. When one of the dancers was conflicted between going to her ballet audition that she'd been dreaming about her whole life, instead of going to a modern dance group competition she had recently taken a liking to, the other dancer questioned her by saying, "What do you really want? Not what the 12-year-old version of you wants, but what do you want now?"

What the message of the film revealed to me is that perhaps I was feeling trapped by some of the goals the 13-year-old version of me wanted and I didn't realise that until then. What I have learnt is that we should not be held hostage by the goals of our younger selves when we can see a better way now. Obviously, there is a disclaimer here. It is important to discern between our dreams and life purposes that may come to us at a young age versus being held by a goal we made years ago that no longer serves us or our purpose.

I also learnt that this feeling of entrapment can also occur if we only have one major goal in life and are sticking to it, even if it no longer serves our purposes.

What I gathered is that we should set many goals and we should review and update them regularly.

I used to love playing the piano for example and took the exams quite seriously. However, I realised it was no longer a strong goal of mine but something I'd like to hear someone else play. So I found another more exciting hobby which was Latin American dancing. I took that seriously too and paid for classes and did performances, and now I just want to dance here and there. I know one day I will get back to it more seriously, just not in this season of my life. I also know that I prefer dancing to playing the piano. What I realised is that I am a creative being and I need a place to express my creativity; the piano was an initial start and then dancing. Ultimately my purpose is to write and tell stories because that is my greatest expression of creativity. Along the way, I know I will dabble into other forms of creativity but if they no longer serve my purpose I am willing to adapt, scratch them out and move on. I hope this illustrates the point.

I now review my dreams and goals as often as possible (daily or weekly) and re-evaluate what is still important or what must be updated, which is okay. I have segmented them too, according to different areas of my life, and have prioritised them from A to C depending on their level of urgency.

Point to ponder

Have you ever felt that life seems to be an arduous road leading to nowhere in particular?

Are you taking a laissez-faire approach or an action-oriented approach towards the plan for your life?

Do you feel held hostage by one major goal or those you set many years ago that no longer serve your purpose?

Write out your reflections:

....

....

....

....

Driving the point home

It is okay and normal to feel like this; we have all been there at some point. Awareness is what starts the process of change. Now the question we must answer is what to do about this realisation. We need to reflect and ask ourselves a few more questions: Since when have we felt like we are on a treadmill going nowhere? Are we willing to change and step off and chart a new path for ourselves? If you are feeling that life seems to be going nowhere in particular, perhaps examine whether you're taking an action-oriented or laissez-faire approach. You may also be feeling a sense of disconnect between what you want for your life and what you currently have.

According to Earl Nightingale, in life, we can choose our own circumstances by making positive choices about what we want, and if we don't, the circumstances we don't want will choose us.[22] Basically, we get to choose where we want to go in life, and that's a liberating process instead of being dragged along the current of life, by other people's choices and other life circumstances. Let's choose an action-oriented life where we get to select what we want to incorporate in our lives, instead of a laissez-faire approach that could take us nowhere.

Another argument for being action-oriented, instead of laissez-faire, is because when we let circumstances or other people dictate the course of our lives, we often do not learn from many of the lessons life is teaching us. This is because we embody a thought process that makes us feel that we have no control, and we end up blaming those around us for our circumstances when in fact we have let them decide. This thought process of blame is poor and is often reinforced when we make excuses and keep complaining about our circumstances. When we also don't realise that we are responsible for our poor thought process, we yet again get stuck in a repetitive pattern where we end up complaining more and blaming others continuously. When we go through such repetitive cycles, this just shows that we may have not learnt the lesson life is trying to teach us. We need to take action to assess our thought process and then action towards changing our way of doing things.

Having a mindset embodying a laissez-faire approach also leads to a self-fulfilling prophecy.

Because as the famous saying adapted from Einstein goes, "if you continue to do what you've always done, you'll get more of what you've got". So if you continue taking a laissez-faire approach to life, letting circumstances and people dictate your path, you will continue to get what you have; whether you like it or not. If you don't like what you currently have, you need to take action to change it towards the things you want in your life.

Key takeaways

So we at the end of the day are responsible for the decisions we make. If we want to change them we need to take action. If we can't change them, we need to change how we think about what's in front of us. So how do we go about knowing where we are headed and taking an action-oriented approach?

Firstly, ask yourself: Do you have your GPS (to the destination that is truly yours), and is it on? A great activity to do, as often as possible is to start working on your 10-year timeline. Draw out on paper ten years and list where you are right now in terms of age, kids/spouses age, career/business, and the lifestyle you have. Then do the same on the other end of the page in terms of what you would like as point B in 10 years to be. How would you like your lifestyle to look like? How much money would you like, as asset income and as active income? How would you like your health to be? Do you want to live in a different place? Travel more? Work in something completely different? Start asking those questions and write down the possibilities.

Then look at the gap and see whether there are any discrepancies. Action will only begin to take place when point A is no longer tolerable and then you will need to take specific steps in the different areas to bring you as close to point B over time. Remember reaching point B takes time and is a process, but each time you work on the 10-year timeline you are taking an action-oriented approach, and you are living in the right direction. The habits and steps you develop due to this will lead you to that path. Therefore, it is important to know where you are now and know where you are going.

Understandably, it can often be difficult to envision a different life than what we have, because perhaps over time we have not practised enough dreaming and thinking beyond our circumstances and comfort zones. A good way to start, before looking at the 10-year timeline is to list several dreams and goals that get you on a positive wavelength. Look at that list as often as possible and you will notice that by writing down what you want, mapping a life around it does not seem too impossible anymore. So, have some dreams and goals and strategies attached, and then take action! A great resource on dream building is Keith Abraham's material on setting out your 100 dreams list, and his books such as *BE!* and *Focus*. That is where I started and I constantly review and revise these dreams. I must say I have ticked off a couple of these dreams on my list already and it's so rewarding.

Remember to dream big too. Writing down goals that seem tangible may sometimes be limiting. These tangible goals usually have actions attached to them that involve something that you already know how to do. Other goals involve something you think you can do. I have learnt that the best goals to go for are those that stretch you, sometimes known as fantasy-type goals. These lead to dreams you really really want but do not know how they will materialise. The art of thinking big and goal setting towards a clearly defined goal involves yet another deep discussion. Books and material that can assist with this are *The Magic of Thinking Big*[23] and Bob Proctor's work on setting clearly defined goals.

Remember:

Think about what you want; don't get stuck on the HOW bit. This is because your reticular activating system in your brain will look for the HOW around you. It's all about allowing yourself to operate from a different frequency and subconscious level. You only need to put together what you want and the HOW will come together, almost subconsciously over time. This is detailed further in the book *The Answer*.[24]

It's okay if you take the unintended path; you can always re-route – at least automatically if you set the destination in the first place.

It's okay to also change a goal if it no longer serves your purpose… that's why you should have lots of them and constantly re-evaluate. Sometimes you have to get closer to a goal to see if it's really what you want. Some people have one or few goals and are more likely to stick to them, even if they no longer serve their purpose. So it is important to adapt as you go.

Most importantly, have fun on the road to you!

ABOUT THE AUTHOR

Photograph by Mohini Pillay

Anna currently lives in Johannesburg, South Africa. Her favourite pastime is watching films, spending time with her siblings, travelling with Grant, and reading anything good she can get her hands on. She loves design and beautiful things. She also enjoys a well-cooked meal, often by someone else. Her dream beach house awaits her along with the characters in her future books. This is her first published book.

Anna would love to help you tell your story through her writing business, where she assists her clients - or people like you - through a systematic process to tell their stories of impact through books.

She would also want to help you or your team uncover your life's story, through personal development coaching or workshops that teach the principles in this book. Her services in this regard will lead you or your team to those pivotal 'aha' moments, that change the way you relate to yourself, your past, and others.

If you or your team would like to get in touch with Anna, you can reach her directly at:

anna@impactstoryteller.co.za

Or send an inquiry for one of her services at:

www.impactstoryteller.co.za

Anna looks forward to hearing from you and being of service to you.

REFERENCES

Endnotes

1   Title attributed to *The Good, the Bad the Ugly,* which is a 1966 Italian epic Western film directed by Sergio Leon.

2   Stanley, A. (2020). *Why Is There Suffering In The World?* Accessed online: https://northpoint.org/messages/messy-middle/why-is-there-suffering-in-the-world

3   Title attributed to *The Secret Life of Words,* a 2005 English-speaking Spanish-Irish drama film written and directed by Isabel Coixet.

4   Florence Littauer (1992) Personality Plus; Strand Publishing

5   Andy Stanley (2011). *The Principle of the Path: How to Get from Where You Are to Where You Want to Be.*

6   Slight play on words attributing the film *People Like Us* - a 2012 American drama film directed by Alex Kurtzman.

7   Slight play on words attributing the film *10 Things I Hate About You* - a 1999 American romantic comedy film directed by Gil Junger.

8   Stanley, A. (2011). *The New Rules for Love, Sex and Dating*. Accessed online: https://northpoint.org/messages/the-new-rules-for-love-sex-and-dating/the-right-person-myth

9   Eggerichs, E. (2004). *Love & Respect: The Love She Most Desires; The Respect He Desperately Needs.*

10 Chapman, G. *The Five Love Languages.* https://www.5lovelanguages.com/5-love-languages/

11 Chapman, G. (2010). *Things I Wish I'd Known before We Got Married.* https://www.5lovelanguages.com/book/things-i-wish-id-known-before-we-got-married/

12 Wright, H.N.. (2004). *101 Questions to Ask before You Get Engaged.* Harvest House Publishers.

13 Stanley, A. (n.d.). *What Happy Couples Know.* Accessed online: https://yourmove.is/category/relationships/

14 Stanley, A. (2011). *The New Rules for Love, Sex and Dating*. Accessed online: https://northpoint.org/messages/the-new-rules-for-love-sex-and-dating/the-right-person-myth

15 Title attributed to the book *Great Expectations* – an 1860-1 novel by Charles Dickens.

16 Title attributed to the film *Hidden Figures* - a 2016 American biographical drama film directed by Theodore Melfi.

17 Slight adaptation attributing the film *Facing the Giants* - a 2006 American Christian drama sports film directed by and starring Alex Kendrick.

18 Slight adaptation attributing the film *Alice Through the Looking Glass* - a 2016 American live-action/animated fantasy adventure film directed by James Bobin.

19   Google Dictionary.
20   Title attributed to the film *Wake Up and Dream* - a 1946 film directed by Lloyd Bacon.
21   Stanley, A. (2011). *The Principle of the Path: How to Get from Where You Are to Where You Want to Be.*
22   Allan and Barbara Pease (2016). *The Answer.*
23   Schwartz, D.J. (1959). *The Magic of Thinking Big.*
24   Pease, A & B (2016). *The Answer.*

www.ingramcontent.com/pod-product-compliance
Lightning Source LLC
Chambersburg PA
CBHW020200090426
42734CB00008B/894